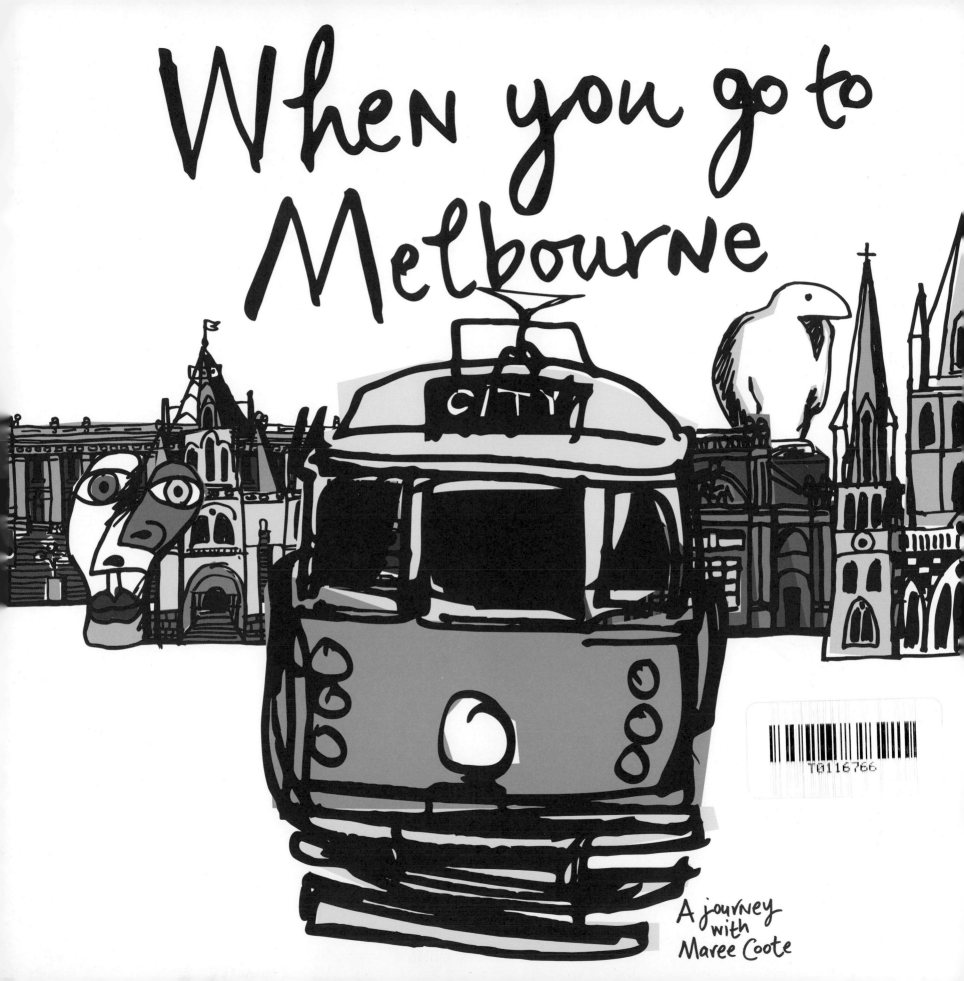

When you go to Melbourne

CITY

A journey
with
Maree Coote

T0116766

When you go to Melbourne,
See if you can see
All the things that I saw
When Mum took me.

Some things there
You won't believe,
But everything is true –
Look up, look down,
Look all around,
And you will see them too.

When you go to Melbourne,
See if you can name
The hundred-year-old buildings
That still look just the same.

See if you
Can understand
The whole tram thing:
Timetable,
Hook turn,
Ticket-pass,
Ding!

When you're there make sure you see
The street art in the lanes –
Sometimes it lasts for ages,
Sometimes just 'til it rains.

When you go to
Melbourne,
See if you can see
Mr Hoddle's
Melbourne Grid
Of eight blocks
By three.

This wooden dress is so uncomfortable.
To think I trained for centuries to end up in a job like this!
I, II, III, IV, V, VI, VII, VIII, IX, X, XI, XII
He's wearing wooden undies!
I should have been back at work X minutes ago!

I like to go to Bourke Street
For my favourite recipe;
Mum likes the top of Collins
Where Le Louvre used to be.

When you go to Melbourne,
See if you can say:
How many bridges between
Burnley and the Bay?

When you finish
Looking 'round,
See if you can see
Where we found
 The rum cakes,
When Mum took me.